# Robinson's Crossing

# Robinson's Crossing

## Jan Zwicky

Brick Books

National Library of Canada Cataloguing in Publication

Zwicky, Jan, 1955-
   Robinson's Crossing / Jan Zwicky.

Poems.
ISBN 1-894078-37-3

I. Title

PS8599.W53R62 2004      C811'.54      C2004-902833-2

We acknowledge the support of the Canada Council for the Arts,
the Government of Canada through the Book Publishing Industry
Development Program (BPIDP), and the Ontario Arts Council for
their support of our publishing program.

The photograph on the cover is "Towards the Porcupine Hills"
by Robert V. Moody.

The book is set in Centaur as interpreted by Monotype. Centaur was
originally designed by Bruce Rogers. Its italic type was designed by
Frederic Warde.

Design and layout by Alan Siu.

Printed on Zephir Antique Book Laid and bound by
Sunville Printco Inc.

Brick Books
431 Boler Road, Box 20081
London, Ontario  N6K 4G6

brick.books@sympatico.ca

We cannot be careful enough in refusing to ... live a split life ... And yet, in many circumstances, we cannot avoid acting as economic men of our time, performing certain professions and thus maiming our hearts. I look at this issue in the perspective of the 'has been', the historian, and in that way [try to] avoid the deforming shadow that the future might throw ...

—Ivan Illich

Each of us, then, should speak of his roads, his crossroads, his roadside benches; each of us should make a surveyor's map of his lost fields and meadows.

—Gaston Bachelard

# Contents

## I

## II

III

I

# Prairie

And then I walked out into that hayfield west of Brandon,
evening, late July, a long day in the car from Nipissing
and long days in the car before that; the sun
was red, the field a glow of pink, and the smell of the grasses
and alfalfa and the sleek dark scent of water nearby . . .
I remember — now — chasing something underneath the farmhouse table as a child
and seeing the big hasp on the underside that locked the two main leaves: it seemed
rough and enormous, out of keeping with the polished surfaces
it held together, almost medieval, I was startled and a bit afraid; and later
as an adult, fumbling for it, blind, at the limits of my reach,
how finally it would let go with a sharp jerk and the leaves
would sigh apart:  but it was there,
in that hayfield, that I felt some rusty weight in my chest stick
then give, a slow opening to sky —

it was that hasp, I know it now,

though at the time I did not recognize I was remembering,
nor, had you told me, would I then have known why.

# Chat

Porch-dweller, afterlife
of all that can be said
when what's been done's
been done, I'll walk you
to the corner store now that the heat's
gone off the day.  Anti-opera,
let me put the kettle on.

May we stay sane, may
the lightning strike
a few feet to the right
or left.
           Lost sister of philosophy,
park my half-ton in the crossroads
and roll the window down.

No rock's worn smooth
by just one wave, but think
how many have washed in
since water was invented.  Tao
of the coffeeshop, exact
inconsequence: over and yet over
the world's dark weedy head.

# Bee Music

Keepers of the secret
sound of sunlight, no job
too small, this
is the cheerful
earless tuning of the music
of the spheres:  O
lunchpail Pythagoreans,
who'd have guessed
the crystal nocturne
of the cosmos was first
scored for miniature
fun-fur kazoos?
Deaf as tiny
Beethovens, you bend
the goldenrod
beneath your weight.
In your toolbox, Euclid
and the sextant of your
sunstone eye.
Ah, little nectar-
mules, you
scholars of the azimuth!  Ah,
perfumed geometers
of the fields!

# Bone Song

Bones, my thanks
for your support,
your efforts to convince the world
that I can stand up for myself.
Thanks for your patience,
and for being home to certainties,
though they are often sad.
For beauty more than
skin deep; for the cheekbone and the pelvis;
for the beauty of horses, thank you.
Also for my love of moonlight,
the dream-case of the skull,
for being moonlight in me,
minarets and tendon-spindles,
labyrinth of the internal ear.
Thank you, especially, for music.
And for the legbone and the thighbone,
for the elegant contraptions

of the wrist and knee, those nuts
and bolts of movement and the root
of how we mean.
Thanks for the orange crate
for my innards, hoop ladder
of the breath, and the reminder
that dying, like everything else,
takes time.
         Blood
believes in busyness
and spring, but you
are winter in us,
ancient ice.
My thanks, white sister,
inner eggshell,
flowering of rock.

# Metaphysics

It was then, the long haul of understanding almost
over — Hume, the Presocratics, and the gaudier
confusions of unbridled sense experience sold off
as kitchen ornaments — we could begin to see
the fruits of all we'd worked towards. At last
wood panelling was sloughing off its grain,
wetness congealed in slicks along the surface of the sea.
We could begin to tell the dancers from their
two-steps, and the two-steps were becoming one
and one.
      Starlight had been sealed
in lead, the stars themselves were being sorted
in denumerable sets along with angels, grains of sand,
and heads of pins. Teeth
gleamed distinct from pointiness; our language
taught us everything we knew. The cats alone
resisted our best efforts, they remained
intractably attached to cat-shapes, but our confidence
was great that in the last analysis, they'd be
revealed.
      By day,
the sky was swirled with green, leaves
leaping from the trees. And while we laboured
through those arc-lit nights, the system
magnified us in its purged electric tongue.

# Epistemology

*If you do know that here is one hand, we'll grant you all the rest.*
—Ludwig Wittgenstein

Because there were no hands, they were
completely absent. I don't mean this as a joke. Nothing
prepared me for it: it was like a dream.
That's why. Because I've tried hard to forget.
And, without warning, I could tell that I was
seven storeys in the air. The fragrance of the earth
when I lay down on it. Because
I'd pulled the fuses from my heart
and every corridor was suddenly ablaze.
Because things like that don't happen on the bus.
I mean that when I stepped out on that plain,
I'd been alone for years — it was
the breath of spring, and it was snowing.
Because it was a river in my heart, because
it moved like winter underneath my skin. A tree
came into leaf behind my eyes.
It woke me up.
The silence sparkled. Imagine
singing without sound, because it was
like that; and when I think of it at lunch,
Liz, Shelley talking about movies, Gerry
hockey, Bruce about the mayonnaise,
I start to cry. Because my body
was a flock of horned larks and my bones were
bells. It didn't care — that's how I knew.
Because it was the opening of an eye. And, yes:
because it was against all reason.

# Theories of Personal Identity

The photograph;
the past life;
the long lost
black sheep who's become
the shoe that fits.
The ghost town,
a.k.a. the rummage bin,
that old sweet song.
The suitcase; the hotel
room; the surprise
box lunch; the plain
brown wrapper. The umbrella
someone opened in the house.
The alphabet, or perhaps
I mean a river, or a well.
The skeleton in the closet.
The writing on the wall.
The telltale heart.

# Soup

.

O, lake of gardens
and with bread
one flesh,
you dwell
in roundnesses,
body of rain.
Not tea,
which throws
the towel
around our neck, says
*get back out there,*
*keep your left*
*up.*
You
say nothing,
make our toes
grow roots.
In stew
is brotherhood,
the warm mess
of connection and
the hide-hung

cave,
but soup,
you give us back
our earth-self
under
open sky.
O, Bolivar
of the sinuses,
Buddha
of the placemat:
you are
that letter
in the mother tongue
we wait for
all our lives.

# Broke Fiddle Blues

Got up this mornin,
> rain pissin down like some monsoon,
Yeah, warm rain in January,
> just like that old monsoon.
They say the climate's changin,
Babe, all my fiddle strings they're outta tune.

Wise lady told me
> folks got rhythm like the trees got leaves.
Wise lady told me (don't you *worry*, girl!)
> folks got rhythm just like trees got leaves.
Don't like this weather, mama,
Muzak never set me at my ease.

Went down to the seashore,
> couldn't hear no rhythm in the waves,
Mmmm down at the seashore,
> wasn't no rhythm in the waves.
Smart folk say meanin's dead,
They're happy shoppin on its grave.

It happened to the jazz man,
> couldn't feel no difference between two & four,

Yeah, it happened to the jazz man (happen to him first, baby),
    couldn't feel no difference between two & four.
Happen to us all, babe, earth don't breathe,
Won't be no music anymore.

Got up this mornin,
    saw my fiddle broke to pieces on the floor,
Got up this mornin,
    yeah, that fiddle it was broke to pieces on the floor.
Leaves turnin yellow in the springtime,
Ain't no exit, baby, cause there ain't no door.

# Mozart and Haydn

Leibniz is famous for the Principle of Sufficient Reason which says you never get two when one will do. And when you think about it, even though at first lots of people can't hear the difference between Mozart and Haydn, and even though Mozart and Haydn hung out in Vienna at the same time, probably ate at the same schnitzelhauses, dedicated string quartets to each other (well, Mozart dedicated some to Haydn), etc. etc., and more or less double-handedly laid down the canonical forms of Western European classical music for the next two centuries — in spite of that, when you think about it, you can see that Leibniz was right, we had to have them both: Mozart, the idiot savant; Haydn, the Zen fool. You listen to an opera like *Marriage of Figaro* — Mozart thinks that true love means having to say you're sorry; but once you say it, no matter *what* you've done, you get forgiven. Haydn's not so sure sexiness is next to saintliness, but he'll bring you chicken soup if you get sick. When someone farts, Mozart gets the giggles; Haydn remembers he had beans for lunch. It's as though Mozart can relieve us of being human for a while, but Haydn knows being human is all we've got. When God spoke to Mozart, Mozart took dictation and didn't miss a syllable. When God spoke to Haydn, Haydn, like the rest of us, didn't understand, but he knew what he had heard was, and was not, the answer.

# String Practice

The fingers of the left hand
are the chambers of the heart.
The thumb is character.
The heart alone
is voiceless.  By itself, it knows
but cannot think, and so
it cannot close the door to fear.

Thought is the right arm
and it moves like breath.
The fingers of the right hand
are thought's tendons, which,
with practice, will take root along
the bone of breath.  Breathe
from the shoulder.  It is thought
that pulls the bright gut of the heart
to speech.

        Breathe also
from the knees, which tune
the ear to earth, its turning,
and the double-handed movement
of the day and night.

If the knees are locked
the mind is deaf:
it fills the house with clamour, then,
but never music.

The collarbone
is the lintel of the voice,
and the breastbone
bears its weight.
In their house, the heart lives
and the breath that is not bone
until thought touches it.

These are the elements,
which is to say,
the difficulty.
When we lack experience,
it is the motions of the heart
that most perplex us.
But of all these things
thought is the hardest,
though its beauty is a distant river
in its plain of light.

# Shabbiness

Not much has changed
since the electric was put in,
that round-shouldered Frigidaire
is probably half a century old.
Asphalt siding;
saskatoons and aspen bush and roses
crowding the north side.
The sort of place you might have spent
your childhood in . . . How quiet
now the rest have gone.

Through the wood-frame window,
hayfields, distant sun — the unwordedness
of beauty pressing up
through ordinariness: an elbow
or a knee, the pink skin showing
where the cloth is thin.

# Wolf Willow

                    Once
I walked out in the evening
to the hill's brow: air
a kind of ocean,
the first night currents
velvety and wet,
sharp in the nose
as menthol, or
like distant flute-song,
like the sound of running water
when it can't be seen;
and the day-scents,
jumbled, dissipating
in the long awns
of the light:  rose,
bedstraw, poplar, spruce;
and caraganas, road dust,
field dust, clover;
car exhaust and cut grass,
dog hair and manure — and then
the dark viola
of your fragrance:  sweeter

than allspice, heavy
as a hank of hair,
or as the light
inside the dim folds
of the curtain —
                                once
I woke to a rustle
close above me, faint
glint of a necklace, then
the closing door — it had been
a kiss,
warm, flushed:
o, that perfume!
the tawniness
that wreathed me,
lifted me through dark
like thirst, like
hunger.

# Aspen in Wind

Little tree, tree of slopes and coulees
and wolf-willow scrub, tree of seven
months of winter and a two-week spring,
of childhood and the endless

sky of loss, I've come
for the light in your leaves,
those brief mosaics of starched silk, the rill
and sifting of the August air against

the speechless blue, for this light like light
off water gurgling past the snowbank in the first
real thaw, for shade, for the rest
of weightlessness, I've come

to close my eyes
under the bright wind of summer,
the light-in-water of the wind in your leaves,
the starched silk of their rushing, that quilt

of sorrow and of light.
What is the light for
but to lie down in? What is sorrow for
but to lie down in.

II

# One Version

—after Paul Hindemith, *Funf Stücke*, No. 4

Someone walks alone
under the sky. The sky
is grey, like history. The walker
wears an overcoat but it's
no use: the cold
turns to metal in his joints, noiselessly,
the way it slicks the sky.
Nothing moves: the walker,
who is walking, does not move. That's
history for you. Did I mention
that the walker's back
is to us, collar turned up, that he
wears a hat? Still,
we know everything. We have forgotten
when it was we last slept.
Did I mention we have lost
our eyelids. Did I mention
that the distance lengthens
every step, that every step the distance
stays the same.

# Robinson's Crossing

They say
the dog was crazy that whole evening:
whining at the door, tearing
around the yard in circles,
standing stock still in the cart track,
head cocked, whimpering.
They'd left him out and gone to bed, but he
kept barking until after midnight
when they finally heard him take off
down the railbed, east,
toward the river. Next morning
Ernest said he'd met him
a half-mile from the house. The train
had got in late but he'd
been eager to get home, so walked
the eight miles from the crossing
at the steel's end. They had finished
with the harvest down south, he had money
in his pocket. He was
two days early,
but the dog had known.

My great-
grandmother slept

in a boxcar on the night
before she made the crossing. The steel
ended in Sangudo then, there was
no trestle on the Pembina, no siding
on the other side. They crossed
by ferry, and went on by cart through bush,
the same eight miles. Another
family legend has it that she stood there
in the open doorway of the shack
and said, "You told me, Ernest,
it had windows and a floor."

                The museum
has a picture of the Crocketts —
later first family of Mayerthorpe —
loading at the Narrows
on the trail through Lac Ste. Anne.
Much what you'd expect:
a wagon, crudely covered,
woman in a bonnet on the box seat,
man in shirt sleeves
by the horses' heads, a dog.
But what draws the eye, almost
a double-take, are the tipis

in the distance, three of them,
white, smudged — a view the lens
could not pull into focus.
And another photo,
taken in the '30's maybe,
of a summer camp down on the river flats
between our quarter and the town.
At least a dozen tipis; horses, smoke.
By the time I was a kid,
they'd put the town dump there;
but I remember we picked arrowheads
out of the west field every spring
when it was turned.  And a memory
of my uncle, sharp, impatient with
my grandfather for lending out
his .22 to Indians:
last time, didn't he remember?,
he never got it back.


                    Robinson's Crossing
is how you come in to this country, still —
though it's not been on a map
since 1920, and the highway
takes a different route.  You come in,

on the backs of slightly crazy Europeans, every time
you lift your eyes across a field of swath
and feel your throat catch
on the west horizon.  It's the northern edge
of aspen parkland, here —
another ten miles down the track,
the muskeg's getting serious.
But my great-grandfather was right:
cleared, seeded, fenced,
trees left for windbreaks and along
the river's edge, it looks
a lot like England.
You could file
on a quarter section for ten dollars;
all you had to do to keep it
was break thirty acres in three years.
The homestead map shows
maybe two in three men
made it.  Several of their wives
jumped from the bridge.

                There's no mention
in the local history book

of how the crossing got its name.
I found a picture of an Ernie
Robinson — part of a road gang
in the '20's — and of an old guy,
Ed, at some town function
later on.  There's also
a photo of a sign, undated, shot
from an extreme low angle, as though
whoever took it had been standing
in the ditch beside the grade.  I'll show you
where it was:  just go out
the old road from the RV park, west,
about two miles.  Nothing there now
but a farmer's crossing and a stretch
of old rail in the ditch.  I'm guessing
that they closed it
when the steel moved on
after the war.

                    A few years back
I was out behind the old house
picking twigs.  (TransAlta

had come in and taken out
a poplar — it had left
enough junk in the grass
my mother couldn't mow.)
The rake had clawed
the grass out, more than
it had piled up twigs,
so I was squatting, sorting
dirt and grass by hand.  The smell
was mesmerizing:  musty, sweet,
dank, clay-ey; green —
and with a shock I realized
what it was:  the same smell
as my family.  Not because
our boots and gloves
were covered in it, nothing
you could shower off — it was
the body's scent, the one
that's on the inside
of your clothes, the one a dog
picks up.  Our cells were
made of it:  the garden, and the root

cellar, the oats
that fed the chickens, and the hay
the steers.
                    These days

the line north of the farmhouse
carries only freight,
infrequently; the highway's
being twinned; Monsanto
just released another herbicide-resistant
seed. Before the drought,
the river flooded every time it rained —
no trees upstream; this year
it's lower than it's been
since someone started
keeping records. The wooden
elevators, gone or going; ranks
of concrete silos that read
*Agricore* in flowing nineteenth-century
script — it's why

the story matters, why it
puzzles me. Here comes

my great-grandfather, he has made
Robinson's Crossing, he is walking
toward us, bone-tired
but whistling, it's a fine night, he has
money in his pocket,
and the dog, the family dog,
is going out to meet him.

# History

—after Béla Bartók, *Divertimento for Strings*, Sz. 113

Someone is sitting in the small glow
of a fireplace.  Earlier, when he looked out,
he could see the smoke, like overweight
black party-streamers,
and the usual rubble in the street.  Now
his desk is locked; yesterday
he burnt the fly-leafs from his books.

In a lull, he hears a rustling
in the cupboard, then a little *tink*.
A mouse has found the cheese rind
from his breakfast.  It is bold,
this mouse, and merely steps back
one or two mouse-paces while the man
divides what's left.  The armies

are marching in the bathroom now,
the basement.  The mouse
settles on the broad rim of the plate
to eat its portion.  Elbow on a shelf,
the man eats standing up.

# Track

Legend has it I was two and blonde
and sullen when my grandmother
arrived to meet us at the station,
and my first words to her came
some twenty minutes later as the hunch-backed Ford
slewed through the eight-inch ruts:
"Jesus Murphy!" I'm reported
to have hollered from the back seat,
"Watch out for the mud!"
                                        Later,
my childhood beginning to congeal
around the things I said about it
like gumbo on an unscraped boot,
I would object again: not to the mud, but to the re-
routing the county had insisted on
before they'd give us gravel. The new road
didn't use the bridge, but crossed the river at the sluice
on 22, and churned
inelegant and graceless up the rise
past Adams'. Nothing in it of the path
or track — no caress
of contour, no interest
in its difficulties. But what
were those difficulties? Did I

know?  Even as I fumed
about the new road, I'd have told you
that the old one didn't lead to any place
you'd care to go.
                                    And even later,
we're going through old pictures with my grandmother
at the Lodge — the strokes
have left her timid and uncritical, suddenly
bewildered, desperate to staunch
the haemorrhage of memory.  "Where
was that taken, then?  On BB's place?"  "No, that's
the north field."  "You mean
the hay meadow?  Behind the barn?  But where's
the lane?"  "The lane?  It didn't
go in till the '40's."  "The '40's!
Then how'd you get to town?"  "Oh.  Well . . ."
and she drifts off in confusion
so I have to ask my mother
on the way home.  It's hard work,
she's sharp, dismissive, won't elaborate
unless I prod.  But it turns out
the first road from the house
struck off down through the west field
— in the wrong direction! — used
the road allowance bridge to cross
the river and then the grid

to get to town.  Some flood
took out the bridge, so Charlie put a culvert
in the creek behind the barn
and they went east. When they got the Model T,
they still went east, but ducked
beneath the trestle to the bridge.
The road I grew up with, to Greencourt,
went in as part of the Alaska Highway
in the war:  that's when, she says,
they built the lane.

             And now, in the twilight,
leaning on the open garage door — my mother
gone inside, water running in the kitchen, then
the phone, two rings, her voice
low, barely audible — I find myself remembering
one afternoon, a trip through the sand hills north
of Blue Ridge, stopping for a pee
and noticing a track and following
it up through scrub to the remains
of an old homestead.  Fifty years, I guessed,
but knots of roses, tangled, wild, still tracing
what had been the lane or possibly
a path down to the barn.

                And it's true
that when I was a kid
there still were pilings in the river

from the road allowance crossing,
down the west field: but no sign
there might have been
a track from the direction of the house.
I went down to stare
often enough — my first ruin —
I would have noticed.
You can see, too, where the culvert
must have been, north-east
of the barn.  But again, there's no trace
up the east field, even in
the aerial farm photographs.  When I ask her
why it doesn't matter to her
everything has changed,
she shrugs.  "We did
what we had to do
to get there."

> — *like the time*
> *when Charlie Pat phoned to say he'd seen*
> *Mrs. Trimbell out there in the blizzard*
> *with no coat and her two kids, crazy, maybe*
> *heading to our place and Charlie*
> *hitched the sleigh up and went out*
> *to find them.  And the time*
> *Jean had the whooping cough,*

*Marie had walked the trestle for the doctor*
*but when he tried to walk it with her,*
*couldn't take the vertigo, had*
*to crawl back on his hands and knees and go*
*the long way round. The famous*
*Model T that made it up the famous*
*muddy hill; the engagement ring,*
*lost in the winter,*
*maybe when Marie was opening*
*the east field gate —*

                              but as she says

why does it matter to me
now? —They're myths, the history gone
the second that it happened.
And I'm as tired as she is
of happy times down on the farm,
and just as tired of all those blood-and-guts
home truths, the stupid
gothic grab of land and family, stuff
her generation thought
unspeakable and mine
turned into books.

                    But I guess I think
it's still another kind of craziness
to wipe the map

clean, give up
that part of who we are that's
what connects us —
                    as though
it would be unimaginable:
some track that's always been there,
rose-edged, trailing off at dusk down to the river,
some different set of stories
we don't know how to tell.

# History

—after Joseph Haydn, Op. 64, No. 2, Adagio

It's quiet now.
The nameless officers for State Security
shrug on their overcoats
and head home through the pre-dawn streets.
Oiled locks turn,
then turn again.
The generals snore.
Now light comes.
You will think it cold,
the way it fingers
open eyes, the darkened cheekbones,
the blood between the legs.
You will think it deaf as generals
the way it stands beside the ones still dying
and moves on.
But see
how weightlessly it gathers them,
the gold curl and the ebony,
with what tenderness
the folded silence of the ribs.

# Nostalgia

Dusk falling, late afternoon, mum
off at the nursing home, I'd been
sorting stuff all day:  plastic
couch-leg coasters, old
prescription vials, walnut-and-pipecleaner
Christmas ornaments, and then
bobbing up in all that
under-the-basement-stairs clutter,
you: the sudden lurch,
a kind of memory
shock, shift
to a real past tense.
What were you doing there?
Other stuff from the old place
she'd kept upstairs, on view.
Heavy in the hand, oddly
companionable — I stared
then put you in my pack
and took you home.

But now,
unsettled by my need, uncertain what it was
I recognized, it's embarrassing
that you're a clock.  All those clichés —
old ticker, stopped short, *neiges d'antan* — not
what I want.  In fact

you go just fine:  the feathered ratchet as
the key turns in your gut, the tiny precise
*cluck* of your mechanism,

                            *yes,*

                                    *how quiet*

        *that small parlour,*
        *curtains drawn against the summer*
        *heat, the doilies motionless*
        *on end tables, on the backs of chairs,*
        *those round, green-centred peppermints*
        *in an Indian brass bowl,*

                            not time, then, or not
exactly — you name some other loss, some
stillness, some thing inside the stillness
of that room:  not memory, but
perhaps what memory's for.

                            *Seams*

        *in her stockings and the black*
        *laced pumps, skirt*
        *of her shirtwaist falling*
        *mid-calf — bluish grey*
        *seersucker (or was that*
        *the asphalt siding*
        *on the house? — same grey, as I*

*remember, and half*
*the buildings in the country*
*covered in it); iron smell*
*from the water on the wash stand,*
*wood-ash from the cook stove, and the dim length*
*of the kitchen, just*
*the corner windows at the northwest end;*
*the little bookcase by the*
*entrance to the parlour, and the picture*
*hung above it in a narrow frame:*
*a cutout in black paper*
*set against a coloured print of steepled*
*countryside, and magically*
*the silhouette of a young woman runs*
*in the lacey shade*
*of English trees . . .*


                      And the surprise
I wanted anything:  not always
so.  But now, the more
they die off, and the more stuff
gets consigned to the museum
or the dump, the more the things
I find myself remembering
are sweet.  Or, no:  it's that

they're not hoared with
unhappiness. And yet, not just
that either: full
somehow — but full of what?
The images swim up, sharp,
fragranced, but — like you —
behind a pane of glass.

         *Or later*
    *lying on the bed upstairs, deep*
    *afternoon, a faint scent from the black spruce,*
    *crosshatch of the screen set in the window; shadiness, the shadow*
    *of the room, and faint, faint, something*
    *stirring, hardly a breath, less than my*
    *breathing . . .*
              Is it
my childhood that I'm missing then?
Not in the basement with the clocks.
Where has it gone, why now
be wanting it?
             *. . . a silhouette*
      *of English trees, the doilies*
      *on the mantelpiece, blinds drawn . . .*
                And why
that room, your measured tick, the picture
on the threshold of that summer afternoon? Why not

her kitchen table, or her plates, the cups
of tea?  That's mostly
where we would have spent
the time, invited in for cake or squares
after we'd done our chores and
washed up in the main house.  (How
bewildering, it strikes me now,
we must have seemed:  our jeans,
our appetites, our
brute, unenglish curiosity.)

A ghost that hovers just above the tongue.
It's not my childhood
but the place it's gone
that I can't get to.  Something
inside the shroudedness, a holding
still:  what history isn't,
but the silence in between the ticking
is.  Because what would I say
if I could walk into that kitchen now?  It's true
some days I can't breathe for
the sad smoke of the endings
that we engineer, but the past's
no better:  three parts
colonial brutality to two parts

purple gas exhaust —
                         it's loss
itself I've lost, I think:  the distance
of the present from some steadiness I didn't know
I loved.  And there's no cardboard box
under some flight of cosmic stairs,
no set of shabby metal shelves,
where I might look.  Meaning
has the night shift, but the place
is empty and nobody really cares
if it shows up.  The urge it has sometimes
to do the old soft shoe,
or weep.  If it could get behind
the pane of glass, if it could make change
real, be owned
by what time moves through,
not by time.

> Like the faintest of breezes,
> midafternoon silence, my face
> to the window, the curtain
> just stirring ... Where is it,
> your childhood? faint lifting, faint
> stirring ... Not even
> this stillness, not even
> this breath.

# History

—after J.S. Bach, *Concerto in D Minor*, BWV 1052

Someone is running
fingers through their hair.
The fingers
are like fish, they flicker
upstream while the current
purls around their backs
and falls away.
The fish

resemble wind inside a field
of wheat, resemble
solar flares, the fish
are water
that is trying to flow
up itself, the gravity
that hauls and tumbles it

deaf as the grief
inside perfection.
Do not ask.
You are running fingers
through your hair. This
is what you do sometimes
because you cannot put your hands
around your heart.

# Black Spruce

A late-May evening, the fields straw coloured, only a touch of green ghosting the pastures because of the drought. The tuft of aspens on the gravel bar just coming into leaf in the last day or so, late, because of the cold. The soil in my mother's garden looks like black face powder — as though, if you touched it, it would feel that fine. Bits of dried peatmoss collect in the depressions of rows where beets and carrots have not sprouted. It's always windy now, she tells me; and cold; and overcast — though never any rain.

I'm out walking after supper. As often on a cloudy day, the sun has broken through as it drops west, and the winter-white stubble glitters in the low-angled light. The clouds begin to break up, rifts of blue opening between the great swales of the cyclone slowly churning its way out of the northwest. As it sets the stubble gleaming, the sunlight also seems to loft the dark underbellies of the clouds higher, firing their crests a dense, incandescent white. The air is sharp with shadow and with light.

A stretch of river glints up across the flank of the west field. It was visible as soon as I stepped through the windbreak west of the house. This is partly because the foot of the west field sweeps down close to the river and beavers have felled all the aspen and balsam poplar along the river's edge, and partly because, in spite of the drought, the river is exceptionally high:

dammed repeatedly over the course of its meanderings by the same beavers. My mother has warned me there are no fords left.

Even so, I am unprepared for the extent of the change. What used to be a series of clear brown pools linked by rapids of fist- and ostrich-egg-sized stones, is now a thirty foot wide sheet of currentless and cloudy grey. I can see the lip of a dam about thirty yards downstream, and hear the surprisingly loud gush over it. Beyond it, another flat expanse, backed up around the first of two right-angle bends.

The riverbank from the dam to the bend forms the west edge of a little wild area my grandfather never cleared. There's a sink of sorts in the middle which, during the wet years of my childhood, was always squelchy, even in August; and the eastern end rises very steeply to the horse pasture — both good reasons to have left the area in trees, assuming he wanted any beyond the simple beauty of the result. When I was a kid and wanted to be alone, I came down here. Not by way of the open slope of the west field and south along the river as I've come this evening, but less visibly through tunnels in the caragana-and-poplar windbreak, a dash across the north end of the horse pasture, and a plunge into the woods at its easternmost corner. Deer and the dog had worn a trail just along the fenceline — the crest of the steep slope up from the sink. It was rough — there was a lot of deadfall and wild rose and tangly saskatoon-and-poplar-sapling undergrowth — but it was marginally better than bushwhacking. The trail led along south, to just above the second of the right-angle bends, where it petered out, branching along and down toward the river in several directions.

Right on that second bend was a big black spruce. Actually, there were three stems, but I thought of them as one tree. One stuck out from the bank above the water a good foot before shooting straight up; the other two were set back into the bank, leaving a kind of platform of roots and pale clay-ey soil between themselves and the one that stuck out. It wasn't exactly a hiding place — the spruce was so old it had lost its lower branches, so anyone sitting in the middle was pretty visible — but it was a bower of sorts. The other side of the river was too steep to be farmed and so was also wild land as far as you could see in either direction. It was shady, but not dank — sunlight dappled in across the water and filtered down through the dog-tail branches of the spruce. You could sit on the stem that stuck out and dangle your feet in the water. There was a narrow ford just upstream where you could fool around on stepping stones, and once I found a freshwater clam. But mostly I just sat and swatted mosquitoes and did nothing. The rill of the water through the stones was faint, not as loud as the aspens unless the day was very still. Some birdsong —

robins, jays, a song sparrow, chickadees, the occasional wren —
but significantly less than nowadays. We didn't feed — no one
did — and it was the heyday of DDT.

This evening, as I turn from the river toward the woods, it's
clear the beavers have been at work there, too — not just along
the bank, but deep inland. The whole grove looks sparse, and
the closer I get, the worse the damage appears. Three in four
trees are down, in places the sixty-foot trunks toppled, stacked,
criss-crossing, splayed out like a bomb site. A lot of it is very
fresh, some trees chewed through but still standing, balanced on
the pencil-point of heartwood, tilting into a neighbouring tree,
both just coming into leaf. Nearly every sapling has been
taken, too — but in a single, clean upward slice, like an axe-
blade might make. There are beaver slides, heavily worn, every
eight to ten feet along the bank. I can't stop thinking about all
those teeth, how, even while I'm thinking about them, they keep
growing.

Beavers were a rare sight along the river when I was a kid. I
remember being taken down at dusk one summer night — well
after eleven, the whole incident so surreal in memory I may
have been woken up after having been put to bed — and just
making out the wide V, wider than any muskrat's, before the
huge slap startled us all so much we gasped and someone —
Uncle Keith? — slipped in the mud. They have been steadily

growing more numerous over the years. Among other things, they have no natural enemies — we have the odd coyote, but no wolves, and only rarely a bear down from House Mountain to roll in the oats in the fall. I'd been thinking the water couldn't be too healthy for them, what with the pesticides and herbicides used upstream. But maybe the pollution has been making them *more* fertile?

Of course, having seen the levels on the river, and the damage upstream to the soft clay banks, I'm ready for the spruce to be submerged and tilting, possibly even toppled into the river. But when I get around the debris piled up behind the trees still standing near what used to be the ford (there's another dam there, and another, it will turn out, downstream from the next bend, and another, and another after that), there's nothing. The whole hillside has slumped and been absorbed into the river, leaving a cutbank, pale and raw, some fifteen, eighteen feet high. A couple of fenceposts lean drunkenly out from the horse pasture, barely held in place by the barbed wire that once stretched taut between them.

A dissolution that complete, taken by water in a year without rain. The cold weight in the pit of my stomach — something awry where I thought I was least vulnerable, in the place that was stable when other things weren't, that was solace because unchanging, or changing cyclically, slowly, on a rhythm large enough to serve as a backdrop against which other losses might be made sense of, and I am stumbling up through the cutwood, the deadfall and the prickered undergrowth, not crying but suddenly in a hurry, bursting out the northeast corner into the winter-white hayfield, under those dry, swollen clouds, in my home place, lost.

# History

—after Béla Bartók, *String Quartet No. 6*, Sz. 114

Someone is standing
at a wall.  The wall
is high and curves away
on either side, through smoke,
to the horizon.
She has been standing there
some time.  Once
she raised her hand to it
and underneath the glassy surface something
spasmed:  flash of brilliant
blue-green wing;
a severed ear.
A bloodless palm swam up then,
mirror image of her own,
and now the reek
won't wipe away.

At her back
the paths are tumbling
over one another in their
hurry to escape.  Remember,
it is silent.  A shadow
creeps up,

settles on its haunches
by her side.
She cannot look.
She squats, too,
head cocked,
listening.

III

# Another Version

Look, all I can tell you is
there was a car, big, dark blue,
a late-'40's Ford sedan; and rain,
and getting stuck, and rain and rain.
Forcing the back door wide enough
to struggle out, the ruts
shin-high, the gumbo
slick and shiny in the half-light,
gunmetal, the wet-iron
smell of it.
And how it packed itself
like pie dough in the wheelwells,
the scuffed burr of the spinning tires,
the men cursing and grunting as they rocked it,
exhaust thickening the drizzle
and the hubcap logo stopping upside
down, then right side up, then
upside down. And that we had to wait
until the tractor
came: the clank-whump
as the chain drew taut, the lunge,
the heave, the drunken

fishtail as we broke
the suck; and maybe also, thinking
even then that we'd misunderstood,
had failed to grasp the meaning
of that monstrous union between
car and road, its refusal
of intent.
As though they knew, wanted
to save us. And we drove on.

## Closing the Cabin

You can see how it will be:
the stillness in the light,
the vacant squares it makes on the kitchen floor

now the leaves are gone.
The way it gathers the room
into itself: the cups, the empty cuphooks,

the dent in the breadbox — an eloquence
we'll never manage, language
without tense.

Not ours: we speak
and then our lungs fill up with air again.
We're only passing through.

# Night Driving

The sky has left us
and the corn that bent and glittered
in the invisible wind is now itself
invisible.  Our headlights
scoop a tunnel in the dark,
and we drive into it.

It's too late for the radio,
we're out of range.  But sometimes
mist in white skeins lifts
from nowhere, ancient
sorrow, earth
breathing in its sleep.

# Leaving New Brunswick

Just south of Edmundston, we pulled off
to change drivers, take a jog
around the car.  It had been raining
when we started, but there'd been an arch
of clear sky in the north all afternoon; now
we'd arrived.  We'd make Rivière-du-Loup
that night, no problem.
                 I was glad:
I'd hoped that coming back
briefly, years after,
might settle something.
But I'd been skittish,
animal-intent, all week: some
three-legged fox, back in the clearing
where she'd sprung the trap.  And angry
at myself: what did I think
could hurt me now? —An apple tree,
an old house, the red bench
by the back door, the little
piece of bone beside it, dull
in the sunshine.
             I leaned
against the car door, stretching
a cramped right calf.  The sun
was setting, and as I forced
my heel to the shoulder's gravel
I looked up and saw the sky flare

too — torqued ribbons, tossed back
from the sun — like the prairies,
I was thinking, or maybe just
like anywhere.
                    But the hills
I saw then, suddenly, could only be
New Brunswick hills: low, rounded,
steep with hardwoods
rusting into fall — and they exhaled
a rusty light; the sky
was gauzy with it, and the St. John —
mirror-dark, like black pearl — wrapped itself,
a glassy mantle, at their feet.
                              I hardly noticed
getting in the car again, but the highway
was falling into shadow north of Edmundston, leaving
the St. John, picking up
the Madawaska,
                    and then
we were at the border, the box lights
of the transports pulling out from the Irving
in front of us, and at our backs,
those clouds,
                    shrunken now,
dark mauve, melting into colourlessness,
frost coming.

# Another Version

The edges of the blocks
showed faintly. (Overhead
a few dull stars.) Silky
to the touch, like marble,
dry. On some,
small bowls of food.

When I paused for breath
sometimes I'd find another
paused there, too — but really
what was there to say?
As we'd been told we would,
we climbed:

in darkness, into dark.

# Study: Late October

On a day when the news is worse than usual, I head out for
a walk. It's cold. To the west, clouds like gloomy, frightened
meringues shred themselves on a wind we can't yet feel. A few
pellets of snow. In the woods, some leaves hang on, doggedly
yellow, but there's a brown surf underfoot, slick with last
night's rain. Just where the trail drops down to the swamp,
I find a single outsize hickory leaf, grey-green, so thin it's
translucent. One last flock of geese straggles overhead: teeth
in a broken zipper, a row of empty buttonholes. Where
someone has cut an aspen to make the trail, the white slice
gleams in the understory light.

# Rose Lake

The summer my father was ill, he told me that as far as he remembered, he hadn't really felt much when his mother died. At the time, I didn't believe this, figuring he just didn't want to talk about it; but now I've learned a little more about the variety of ways bad news can present itself, it seems quite possible that what he said was true.

He also claimed not to remember much in the way of other things that happened from around that time. A few years earlier, under pressure, he'd given me a quick sketch, but for all intents and purposes, the story picked up in his mid-teens: how unhappy he'd been with his new stepmother, her fawning over him, her cruelty to her own daughters, how he'd more or less run away to summer school in Albuquerque, then gone straight to college, graduated, and ended up working for Shell in Fort McMurray by the time he was nineteen. He'd loved college — that I'd always known — and also the new job, and Canada, in spite of the bugs.

It was my uncle who, after my dad's death, was able to fill in some of what had happened in those pre-teen years. There was a snapshot I'd always been curious about. It's the only one we have in which my dad is older than six and younger than seventeen, but when I'd asked my dad about it, he'd just shrugged. It shows my uncle and my father, roughly nine and seven, bare-chested, deeply tanned, waist deep in water. My uncle's bending forward into the camera, laughing, but my father looks as though the photo's interrupted something: he's squinting over his shoulder, as though the light's too bright, and his mouth is drawn in something that might be anxiety or irritation.

We were sitting on the couch after the memorial service, going through my mother's albums, when we came across the photo. My uncle told me that it had been taken at Rose Lake. After their mother died, he said, their father had abandoned the two boys to the care of his own mother, and himself left town. (This isn't, I should confess, quite the way my uncle put it — but then, he's fiercely protective of his father's memory.) She was a cranky woman, less than delighted with her new responsibilities, and sharply critical both of her son and his two boys. Their father occasionally sent money, but there wasn't much. The ramshackle cabin on Rose Lake, rent free, was a way of stretching a meagre income over the summer, as well as getting the kids out from underfoot. From the sounds of it, the boys were left pretty much to fend for themselves: they spent their days outside — swimming, fishing off docks — came in when they got too cold or couldn't stay awake any longer, fed themselves out of cans or at neighbours when they got hungry. My uncle recalls men coming out to the cabin evenings, occasionally afternoons, smoking and playing cards — there might have been a still — he can't remember now.

We'd closed the album and I was getting up to make some coffee when he added, almost as an afterthought, that a funny thing happened, it might have been the first summer they were there. One of the other boys had gone missing. Nobody recalled under what circumstances — fishing? swimming? out in the woods? — but it being summer and boys being boys, it was a while before anyone became seriously concerned. The men finally mounted a search, but found nothing, and everybody eventually figured that he must've drowned. It was my uncle, in the end, who solved the mystery. He was getting ready to jump off the end of the dock one afternoon when he looked down into the water and saw the white shape suspended there — upright, toes just brushing the bottom, looking up at him, apparently unharmed.

# Work


On Tuesdays,
we would drive into the town.
Small town, long drive.  Sometimes,
there might be something wrong,
a machine part broken or a twitchy
tooth.  But mostly we just picked up
tea and flour and the mail.  For the work
was on us then; we needed
next to nothing:  work
like a spell of good weather
you know is going to hold, that mix
of surprise and deep contentment
in the morning when you draw the blinds:
*of course.*  Something about
the arc of destination, its
updraft of light:  work carries us
the way love can, but with
less sorrow.  That whole summer
I wore mismatched laces in my boots,
one red, one white, because I knew
no order could improve upon
the one that gripped me:  the world
unrolling like a field of daisies
in July, the truckbox full of tinned beans,

bread and beer, the road
tireless in its rise along the cutbank,
seared cries of the cicadas,
the dust, the heat.

# Three Mysterious Songs

*Lost Music*

I was standing at the window,
maybe it was winter,
maybe it was raining.  Anyway,
not pacing anymore.
I hadn't tried the door
in months.
           Who was it, then,
pausing on the other side
and looking in?  That glance,
a firm sweet hand that pulled my gaze
to my own limb; the limb, where
dried, clean, open to the bone,
I saw that wound.

*Music's Breath*


Sorrow, I raise my hands to you.
So little we understand!
I was idling there
among the carved woods and the scented boxes,
and I know that it was love
saw me.  But when it spoke,
it was your voice that said my name.

On the south and east
the house was open to the weather.
We moved inside it
sombrely, like ships,
and did not raise our eyes.
When death came, it came
as wild grass through melting snow,
the punk of spring
aloft in loose-limbed light.
What was it, on that evening,
ran chanting before the wind?
Though the sky was still sullen,
the night stiff with unseen stars.

# Some Years Later

It was late March, I think, or April,
not winter anyway, one of those
end of season gigs, Mozart or Haydn, high
spirits, the way they can get, spring coming,
a small band, good charts.  You were standing
with the huddle of smokers by the stage door, glancing up
laughing as the car pulled out, catching
my eye: fingers to lips, uncharacteristically
hammy — that extravagant kiss as we roared by *see ya*
*tomorrow* — and then the next day — what
was it? flu? or you cut yourself making dinner? anyway
the section reshuffled, and me,
as always, leaving town the week after, it wasn't
until the other day, some years later, I remembered
that gesture — how in fact it had been raining, you there
at the edge of the light, your hand trailing out of the bright pool
into the darkness, the tip
of your cigarette like a tail-light
climbing some distant ridge to the horizon — and realized
it was the last time I saw you.

# Glenn Gould:  Bach's 'Italian' Concerto, BWV 971

North of Superior, November,
bad weather behind, more
coming in from the west, the car windows furred
with salt, the genius of his fingers
bright, incongruous, cresting a ridge
and without warning the sky
has been swept clear: the shaved face
of the granite, the unleafed aspens
gleaming in the low heraldic light, the friend
I had once who hoped he might die
listening to this music, the way
love finds us in our bodies
even when we're lost.  I've known very little,
but what I have known
feels like this: compassion without mercy,
the distances still distances
but effortless, as though for just a moment
I'd stepped into my real life, the one
that's always here, right here,
but outside history: joy
precise and nameless as that river
scattering itself among
the frost and rocks.

# Acknowledgements

My thanks to the journals that first published versions of these poems: *The Antigonish Review, Arc, Descant, The Fiddlehead, Grain, The Malahat Review, Mānoa, Poetry International,* and *Poetry Wales.* "Broke Fiddle Blues" also appeared in *Why I Sing the Blues,* an anthology published by Smoking Lung Press.

"Aspen in Wind" is for Tim Lilburn. "Work" is for Trevor Goward. "String Practice" is for Robert Bringhurst.

This book is for Don McKay.